PROTECTING WHAT YOU'VE EARNED

A Legal Guide to Preserving Wealth, Protecting Your Family, and Planning for the Future

Karla Madrazo Villarreal
Madrazo Villarreal A.P.C.
www.madrazolaw.com

First edition, 2026

Published by Madrazo Villarreal APC.

Chula Vista, California

Cover concept and art direction by Karla Madrazo Villarreal. Interior design and book production by Madrazo Villarreal APC. Illustration concepts and art direction by Karla Madrazo Villarreal..

www.madrazolaw.com

English paperback ISBN: 979-8-9973913-0-0.

English ebook ISBN: 979-8-9973913-1-7.

The people, families, and situations described in this book are fictional composites created for illustrative purposes. Any resemblance to actual persons, living or deceased, or to actual events, is coincidental. None of the case studies in this book describes an actual client or an actual result.

Please see the Legal Disclaimer on the following pages for additional important information.

Legal Disclaimer

This book is provided for general educational and informational purposes only. It is not intended to provide, and should not be relied upon as, legal, tax, financial, investment, insurance, medical, or other professional advice. The discussion of legal principles in this book is general in nature and may not apply to your particular facts, circumstances, or jurisdiction.

Unless otherwise stated, the legal discussion in this book is based primarily on California law as understood at the time of publication. Laws, regulations, court decisions, tax rules, exemptions, filing requirements, and administrative practices may change, and the law may differ in other states, territories, or countries. Readers should not act or refrain from acting based solely on the information in this book.

Reading this book, communicating with the author, visiting the author's or law firm's website, or using any checklist, example, or resource described in this book does not create an attorney-client relationship with Karla Madrazo Villarreal, Madrazo Villarreal APC, or any affiliated attorney or professional. An attorney-client relationship is formed only through a written engagement agreement signed by the attorney or law firm and the client.

The stories, names, characters, and examples in this book are illustrative. Unless expressly identified otherwise, they are fictional or are composites created to explain general concepts. Any resemblance to actual persons, businesses, events, disputes, or circumstances is coincidental. No statement in this book should be understood as a prediction, promise, or guarantee of any particular legal, financial, tax, or personal outcome.

Before making decisions concerning an estate plan, trust, will, power of attorney, health care directive, beneficiary designation, business succession plan, insurance coverage, investment, gift, tax matter, or other significant legal or financial issue, consult an attorney licensed in the appropriate jurisdiction and, when appropriate, a qualified tax, financial, insurance, or other professional who can evaluate your individual circumstances.

The author and publisher disclaim liability for any loss, damage, claim, cost, or consequence arising from reliance on or use of the information in this book to the fullest extent permitted by law.

Dedication

For my Higher Power, to whom I have surrendered my will and my life, and in whose care I continue to find direction.

For my father, Ricardo, who has transcended and remains my greatest example and inspiration; for my mother, Lolita, my beloved companion through a thousand battles, who gave me roots; and for my brother, Ricardo, who shares the history from which those roots grew.

For my daughter, Paulina, who inspires me to persevere and succeed.

For Victoria, my current life partner; and for Po, Cami, and Juanjo, who came into my life and enlarged my understanding of family. You are the reason the words protection, home, and legacy carry such meaning for me.

For Chava, my sponsor and best friend, who has stood beside me with truth when I needed it, patience when I resisted, and wisdom when I was ready to hear it.

And for my clients specially those living with silicosis—and the families who stand beside them. Your courage and trust remind me that what we protect is never merely property. It is time, dignity, love, and the people who will carry our lives forward.

Acknowledgments

I am deeply grateful to the remarkable team at Madrazo Villarreal APC. Your dedication, professionalism, compassion, and unwavering commitment make it possible for us to serve every client with care, dignity, and purpose. This book reflects not only my work, but also the daily efforts of people who believe that practicing law is, above all, an opportunity to serve others.

I am also grateful to the many attorneys, mentors, and legal professionals whose example has shaped my understanding of what excellence, integrity, and service truly mean. I owe particular thanks to the attorneys and staff of Brayton Purcell LLP, whose commitment to their clients and unwavering pursuit of justice have left a lasting impression on my professional life. Your example has challenged me to become a better lawyer, a better advocate, and a better guardian of the trust others place in our profession.

No lawyer is shaped in isolation. We are all the product of the guidance, generosity, and example of those who came before us. Thank you for helping me become the lawyer I continue striving to be every day.

About the Author

Karla Madrazo Villarreal is a California attorney and the founder of Madrazo Villarreal APC, where she helps individuals, families, and business owners protect what they have worked a lifetime to build. She is also licensed to practice law in Mexico, giving her a unique perspective on cross-border legal planning and the needs of families whose lives span both countries.

Throughout her legal career, Karla has represented people during some of the most significant moments of their lives. She has seen firsthand how thoughtful planning can preserve not only wealth, but also dignity, family relationships, and peace of mind. She has also witnessed the unnecessary hardship that often follows when important decisions are postponed or left to chance.

Her professional journey—and the personal challenges that have shaped her along the way—have reinforced one simple belief: the most important decisions we make are rarely about money alone. They are about the people we love and the legacy we leave behind.

This book was born from that conviction.

Its purpose is not to turn readers into legal experts. It is to help them understand the decisions that matter, ask better questions, and take meaningful steps to protect the people and the future they have worked so hard to build.

Beyond her legal practice, Karla is passionate about making the law understandable and accessible. Through seminars, educational resources, and community outreach, she is committed to helping families make informed decisions with confidence rather than fear.

She believes that estate planning is not simply about preparing for death.

It is about creating clarity during life.

It is about protecting the people we love.

And above all, it is an act of stewardship.

Karla Madrazo Villarreal

Attorney at Law – California & Mexico

Founder, Madrazo Villarreal APC

Contents

Introduction

The Moment Everything Changes

Maria stood in her mother's kitchen holding a coffee mug — chipped at the handle, its good-luck-cat design nearly worn away from thirty years of washing — that wasn't worth anything to anyone but her, and realized she had no idea what to do next.

Her mother had died eleven days earlier. The house was quiet in a way it had never been quiet before — not the empty-quiet of an ordinary Tuesday afternoon when her mother was simply out, but a permanent kind, one Maria hadn't yet learned the shape of. The house — the one Maria had grown up in, two miles from where she now lived with her own kids — belonged to her now. So did the accounts nobody had fully explained, a life insurance policy she hadn't known existed until a letter arrived, and a phone call from a cousin already asking, gently, what was going to happen to the house. Her mother had worked as a school administrator for thirty-one years. She had never once used the word "estate." But she had left one anyway, and now it was Maria's to steward, whether she felt ready or not.

Nobody had prepared her for this part. The grief, she had expected, in whatever shapeless way you can expect grief. What caught her off guard was the sheer number of decisions now waiting for her — decisions she hadn't known existed until they were suddenly hers to make, each one carrying weight she didn't feel qualified to hold.

This moment arrives differently for different people. For some, it's a phone call about a settlement that finally closes after years of litigation. For others, it's the wire transfer that lands the week a business sale finalizes, or the day a retirement account crosses a number that used to feel theoretical. For Maria, it was a kitchen, a mug, and a house that needed a decision made about it by Friday.

Different doors. Same threshold.

You might be reading this because a settlement finally closed, or a business you built for decades just sold, or a house that's been in your family for a generation now has your name on the deed. You might have never spoken with an attorney in your life, and the idea of doing so now feels intimidating, unnecessary, or like something other people need. You are exactly who this book is for.

What waits on the other side of that threshold isn't really a legal problem, although it will eventually involve the law. It's a stewardship problem — the sudden, unfamiliar responsibility of protecting something on behalf of the people who depend on you, whether that something arrived through a settlement, a sale, an inheritance, or forty years of quiet, disciplined saving.

Most people meet this moment with a version of the same instinct: get the paperwork done, find the right form, sign something, and make the discomfort of not having a plan go away as quickly as possible.

It's an understandable instinct. It's also the wrong one.

The paperwork was never the point. A living trust, a power of attorney, a beneficiary form — these are tools, and tools only matter in relation to what you're building with them. A document can carry out a decision. It cannot make one for you. The real question isn't which documents you need. It's harder and more honest than that: what do you actually want to happen to the people and things you're responsible for, if you're no longer here to manage it yourself?

That question doesn't come with a form. It has to be worked out — in conversation, in reflection, sometimes in disagreement with the people you love most — before any document can do its job. People do not need more legal documents. They need better legal decisions. The documents come after, as the record of a decision already made with care.

The chapters ahead move in a deliberate order. First, the psychology behind these decisions — why more money produces more decisions, not fewer, and why they're emotional before they're legal. Then the legal architecture itself: trusts, powers of attorney, health care directives, and the quiet mechanics of probate. Then the pressures that most often undo good planning — family, fraud, divorce, liability. Then the particular complexity of blended families and closely held businesses. And finally, how to keep a plan alive for decades, rather than filing it away and hoping it still fits twenty years from now.

One clarification worth making plainly: the legal mechanics discussed in this book — trusts, probate, powers of attorney — reflect California law, since that's the law these principles are built on. If you live elsewhere, treat what follows as a map of the terrain, and confirm the specific roads with someone licensed in your own state.

Maria didn't need a form that Friday. She needed to understand what she was actually responsible for, and what a good decision would look like. That's what the rest of this book is for — not instead of an attorney, but before one, so that when you do sit down with someone qualified, you're asking better questions and making decisions you understand and stand behind, rather than ones you sign because someone told you to.

You may have arrived at this book through a settlement, a sale, an inheritance, or decades of quiet saving. The paperwork ahead will look different depending on which door you came through. The stewardship will not.

Part One: The Human Side of Wealth

Chapter 1 — The Decisions Money Doesn't Make for You

Three weeks after his company sold, Daniel sat in his car in a grocery store parking lot, unable to make himself go in and buy milk.

Nothing was wrong, exactly. The deal had closed cleanly. The wire had landed. His CPA had already sent over a summary, his two cofounders had already started their own next things, and Daniel had spent eleven years building something that turned out to be worth exactly what it was worth. He should have felt something like triumph.

Instead he felt something closer to vertigo. Not because the number was hard to understand — he'd built spreadsheets far more complicated than this one — but because the number had, overnight, turned a hundred small decisions that used to answer themselves into open questions. Did he still need to work? Should he tell his parents the real figure, or a smaller one, so they wouldn't worry, or ask? What did he owe his brother, who'd lent him four thousand dollars in year two and never once brought it up since? Was he the kind of person who hired a wealth manager now, or did that make him someone he didn't recognize?

He sat in the parking lot for eleven minutes. Then he went in and bought the milk, and put off the rest.

Daniel's problem wasn't a lack of information. He had capable advisors, more financial literacy than most people his age, and no shortage of resources to solve any single, isolated problem in front of him. His problem was that wealth hadn't simplified his life by removing decisions. It had done almost exactly the opposite.

Before the acquisition, most of the questions crowding that parking lot didn't exist for him, because they had nothing to attach to. You cannot decide how much to give a sibling who asks for help if you have nothing to give. You cannot worry about who inherits a house you don't own, or what a lawsuit might take from you, or whether people are being kind to you for the right reasons, if there is functionally nothing at stake. Modest, ordinary means don't only limit resources — they also limit the number of live, urgent decisions a person has to make about those resources. For most of Daniel's life, the answer to what he should do with his extra money had been simple, because there wasn't much of it.

Wealth — however it arrives, a sale, a settlement, an inheritance, four decades of disciplined saving finally crossing a threshold — doesn't just add resources. It adds an entire category of decisions that were previously theoretical, and it adds most of them at once, usually without warning, to someone who has had no practice making any of them. That's the part almost nobody prepares you for. You don't get better at these decisions by being smart or capable in the rest of your life. You get better at them by making them, and the whole difficulty of this moment is that you haven't had the chance to yet.

Most of these new decisions, on inspection, aren't really about money at all. They tend to sort into three older, smaller questions.

The first is about who you are now — and who you might get to become. Wealth changes, or threatens to change, how you see yourself: whether you're still the same person who grew up without much, whether hiring help means becoming someone else, whether wanting to enjoy any of it is generous to yourself or a betrayal of how you got here. It's also, more hopefully, the first real chance some people get to ask what they'd choose to do with their days if the answer weren't dictated by necessity. That hope can feel almost as unsettling as the fear does. It's a lot of freedom to suddenly be responsible for.

The second is about who you owe. Family, in particular, doesn't wait for you to feel ready. A sibling asks for a loan. A parent needs help they're too proud to request directly. A friend mentions, almost in passing, an opportunity that happens to need exactly the amount you happen to have. Each of these is a small test of a much larger question: what do you actually owe the people who knew you before any of this, and how do you honor it without losing everything you built.

The third is about what outlasts you. Underneath the immediate questions sits a quieter, longer one: what happens to this after you're no longer the one managing it? Most people push this one down the furthest, because it requires imagining your own absence, which nobody enjoys doing on a Tuesday. It's also the one the rest of this book spends the most time on, because it's the one a good legal strategy can help with directly.

Fear runs underneath all three, less like a fourth category than like the current that makes the other three harder to sit still in. Fear of choosing wrong. Fear of being asked and saying no. Fear of being asked and saying yes to the wrong thing. Fear, more than any specific figure in an account, is usually what's actually parked in the grocery store lot.

Recognizing which of the three you're facing matters practically, not only emotionally, because each one calls for a different kind of help. A question of identity is rarely solved by a document; it's better served by a conversation with a therapist, a mentor, or simply time. A question of obligation needs the person you owe, directly, not an intermediary. Only the third question — what outlasts you — is the one an attorney can actually help carry. Bringing the wrong kind of help to the right question, or no help at all, is how most of these decisions stall.

> ***Attorney's Perspective:*** *The clients who take longest to move aren't the ones with the most complicated finances. They're the ones who haven't yet said a word like "inheritance," "trust," or "settlement" out loud to the people it will actually affect. The freezing rarely has much to do with the law. It has to do with a conversation the law is waiting on.*

Daniel didn't work any of this out in the parking lot. It took him closer to four months, and a second, more useful kind of freeze. His wife asked him one night, clearing plates from dinner, what they were actually going to do with the money — not the tax structure, not which advisor, just what they wanted their life to look like now — and Daniel sat there long enough that she put the plates back down. He didn't have an answer. Realizing that was the thing that finally clicked. Every decision he'd been avoiding belonged clearly to one of the three questions above, and he'd been treating all of them as equally urgent, when almost none of them actually were. Whether he still needed to work wasn't a today decision, though it was the loudest one. What he owed his brother wasn't a today decision either — his brother, notably, had never once asked. The one thing that actually was time-sensitive — a beneficiary form his old employer had defaulted years earlier to an ex-girlfriend he hadn't spoken to since college — he'd been ignoring for four months, buried under the weight of questions that only felt more pressing.

Sorting the real decision from the noise around it turned out to be most of the work. The legal tools in the rest of this book — trusts, powers of attorney, beneficiary designations, the rest — are built to answer specific pieces of the third question, what outlasts you. But they only work once you've done the sorting Daniel eventually did: separating what's actually urgent from what only feels that way, and naming, out loud, which of the three pulls is the one actually running the show.

Sorting the Real Decision from the Noise

A short checklist, worth returning to whenever a new decision about money arrives and feels heavier than it should:

- Is this decision actually urgent, or does it only feel urgent because it's new?
- Which of the three — who I am now, who I owe, what outlasts me — is really driving my hesitation?
- Have I said this out loud to the people it affects, or only decided it alone, in my own head?
- Is there a smaller, genuinely time-sensitive task hiding underneath the larger question I keep avoiding?

Reflection

Think of your own version of Daniel's parking lot — the moment a decision about money felt bigger than the number attached to it. What were you actually afraid of in that moment: who you'd become, what you owed someone, or what happens after you're gone? Naming it precisely is usually the first real step toward making it smaller.

The Difficult Question

Of the three questions this chapter describes — who you are now, who you owe, what outlasts you — which one have you been avoiding the longest, and what has that avoidance already cost you?

Part Two: The Architecture of Protection

Chapter 2 — Why a Trust, Not Just a Will

Renata had a trust. She'd been telling people that for three years, ever since the judgment from her case came through and she'd sat down with an attorney to get everything in order. She had the binder to prove it — a thick document with her name on the cover, notarized, official-looking, kept in the same drawer as her passport.

What she didn't have, though she wouldn't find this out for two more years, was a house that actually belonged to the trust. The deed to her home still read her name alone, exactly as it had before she'd ever walked into that attorney's office. The trust existed. It just didn't own anything.

This is, by a wide margin, one of the most common and expensive mistakes in estate planning, and almost nobody makes it on purpose. It happens because signing a trust document feels like finishing a task, when it's actually closer to opening a container. The document creates the container. The trust can govern only the assets properly connected to it, and different assets are connected in different ways. A home, an ordinary bank or brokerage account, or a business interest may need to be retitled or assigned; retirement accounts and some other assets usually require coordinated beneficiary planning instead. Skip that funding and coordination step, and even a well-drafted trust may do little for the assets it never reaches.

To understand why this matters, it helps to understand what a trust is actually built to do, and why it's different from a will.

A will is a set of instructions that takes effect once, at death, and only after a court confirms it's genuine and supervises its execution. That court process is probate. Everything you own in your own name when you die generally has to pass through it before it reaches the people you intended, whether or not you have a will. Probate is a matter of public record, and it typically takes the better part of a year, often considerably longer. Not everything requires it, though — beneficiary designations, survivorship ownership, and California's own simplified procedures for smaller estates can route specific things around probate entirely, worth confirming with an attorney rather than assumed from the estate's size alone. In California specifically, the fees attorneys and executors are entitled to collect are set by statute as a percentage of the estate's appraised value, not by actual hours worked: four percent of the first $100,000, three percent of the next $100,000, two percent of the next $800,000, and smaller percentages as the estate grows from there. That percentage is calculated on the estate's full value before subtracting any mortgage, which means a large, mortgaged property can generate fees well out of proportion to the actual work involved. A court can approve additional fees for genuinely extraordinary work, but the baseline is set by size, not complexity.

A living trust works differently, and earlier. You create it while you're alive, you typically serve as your own trustee, and — this is the part Renata's binder never got to — you connect the appropriate assets to it in the way each asset requires. The trust holds legal title to property transferred to it, but as long as the trust is revocable and you're the trustee, you keep the same practical control and use you had before. Nothing about this arrangement puts your own assets out of your reach; it changes how ownership and succession are handled, not who is in charge day to day. When you die, your successor trustee can step in and administer the assets the trust actually governs, without first asking a probate court to transfer those assets into the trust.

The part almost nobody mentions, because probate avoidance gets all the attention, is that a properly funded trust also solves a problem a will can't touch at all: incapacity. A will has no power until you're gone. If you're alive but unable to manage your own affairs — after a stroke, in the middle of a long illness, during any period where you simply can't sign things or make decisions — a will does nothing, because it isn't operative yet. A funded trust, by contrast, already has a successor trustee named and ready, with a mechanism — spelled out in the trust itself — for that person to step in without a court-ordered conservatorship. The exact hand-off depends on how the trust is written; many require a written medical determination, or some other specific step, before the successor trustee's authority actually begins. That's still a private process, resolved between the trustee, a doctor, and paperwork the trust already anticipated — not a public court proceeding, and not something that has to start from zero the way a conservatorship does. The mechanism that protects your family after you die is the same mechanism that protects you while you're still here but unable to act.

None of this makes a will unnecessary. A well-designed trust-based plan ordinarily includes what's called a pour-over will — a short will whose job is to catch assets that were left outside the trust and direct them toward it through the applicable estate process, and to nominate a guardian for minor children, which a trust document doesn't do. The trust is the main structure. The will is the backstop, not a competitor to it.

> ***Attorney's Perspective:*** *The single most common phone call I get isn't "I don't have a trust." It's "I have a trust — so why is this house still in probate?" The document was never the problem. The forgotten paperwork afterward always is.*

A note for anyone with property outside the United States: a trust created under California law doesn't automatically control, or avoid local succession proceedings for, real property located in another country. Whether it can hold, receive, or transfer that property at all depends entirely on the other country's own property, recording, and succession laws — some countries recognize a foreign trust's authority over local land, many don't, and the rules vary enormously. Property outside the country almost always needs its own, separate plan, coordinated with an attorney who understands both systems, not an assumption that the plan built here automatically extends across the border.

Renata's gap surfaced when her mother needed emergency surgery two states away, and Renata needed to sell a small rental property quickly to help cover it. The title company called two days before closing: the property was still in Renata's name, not the trust's, and someone needed to fix that before anyone could sign anything. Renata read the email twice before it landed — that the trust she'd paid for and kept in a drawer for three years had never actually touched the one thing she now urgently needed it to. Nothing about the sale was actually blocked — it just needed an extra signature and a short delay while the paperwork caught up to what everyone had assumed was already true. It was a manageable inconvenience in that moment, precisely because Renata was alive, well, and available to sign whatever was needed. Had the same gap surfaced after her death, or during a period when she couldn't sign anything herself, her family would have been looking at exactly the probate process, and exactly the incapacity gap, the trust was supposed to prevent. The container had been sitting empty the whole time. Renata just happened to find out while she could still do something about it.

Is Your Trust Actually Funded?

If you already have a trust, this is worth checking today, not eventually:

- Does the deed to your home name the trust, or does it still name you personally?
- Have your ordinary bank and brokerage accounts been titled or otherwise coordinated with the trust as your plan requires — while retirement accounts and other beneficiary-based assets are handled through the appropriate beneficiary forms?
- Does a pour-over will exist alongside the trust, and does it name guardians if you have minor children?
- If you own anything outside the United States, has that been addressed in a separate plan?

- Has anything changed since you signed it — a marriage, a divorce, a new child, a move to a new state, a new property — that the trust hasn't caught up to yet?

Reflection

If you have a trust, when did you last confirm — not assume, confirm — what's actually titled in its name? If you don't have one yet, what's actually stopped you so far: the cost, the paperwork, or simply not knowing where to begin?

The Difficult Question

If you were unable to manage your own affairs tomorrow — not gone, just unable to act, for six months — would the people who love you be able to step in immediately, or would they need a court's permission first?

Chapter 3 — Who Decides When You Can't

Carol had been married to Frank for thirty-four years, most of them spent doing exactly what you're supposed to do: paying down the mortgage, maxing out his 401(k) most years, avoiding debt, retiring on schedule. There was no dramatic windfall in their story, just four decades of consistent, unglamorous saving that had, by their early sixties, become a genuinely comfortable retirement.

Then Frank had a stroke on a Tuesday morning, mid-sentence, while Carol was in the next room.

He survived, and would eventually be mostly fine. But for the first several weeks, he couldn't speak clearly, couldn't sign his name, and couldn't tell anyone what he wanted done about anything. Carol discovered, over the course of one very long week, that being married to someone for three decades gives you almost no legal authority over their individual accounts. Their joint checking account, she could manage without any trouble. His retirement account, held in his name alone, because that's simply how 401(k)s work, she could not touch — not to help pay the mortgage, not to cover his hospital bill, not for anything — without either his signature or a court's permission.

Neither was available. Frank couldn't sign. And nobody had ever given a court a reason to grant Carol permission for anything, because nobody had ever asked.

> ***Myth:*** *A power of attorney is something you eventually get around to once you're older.*
>
> ***Reality:*** *Incapacity doesn't check identification first. Strokes, serious accidents, and complications from routine procedures happen at every age. The paperwork matters exactly as much at thirty-five as it does at seventy-five — the difference is how many thirty-five-year-olds assume it doesn't apply to them yet.*

A durable power of attorney gives someone — your agent — legal authority to handle financial and legal matters for you. Depending on how it is written, that authority may begin immediately or only after incapacity. The word durable is doing real work: without durable language, the authority can end when you become incapacitated, at precisely the point this kind of planning is meant to help.

There are two common ways to structure when your agent's authority actually begins. An immediately effective power of attorney gives your agent authority as soon as you sign it, whether or not you're currently capable of managing things yourself — unsettling to some people at first, though in practice it simply means the authority is already in place the moment it's needed, with no extra step required. A springing power of attorney, by contrast, only takes effect once a doctor, or sometimes two, certifies that you're incapacitated. It sounds more cautious. In practice, it can introduce exactly the kind of delay Carol ran into — finding the right doctor, getting a certification, then persuading a bank the paperwork is sufficient — at the moment speed matters most.

California has specific formal requirements for a valid power of attorney — properly signed, dated, and either notarized or witnessed — so a document that looks complete but skips a step may not actually hold up when someone needs to rely on it, which is one more reason to have it properly prepared and easy to produce well before a crisis, not during one.

Without any power of attorney in place, Carol's practical legal route was a conservatorship: a court proceeding to have herself formally appointed to manage Frank's affairs. That requires medical evidence, a court hearing, and, in California, ongoing reporting back to the court afterward, sometimes for years, at the family's expense. It's a public process, and rarely a fast one. In a situation like Carol's, a properly executed power of attorney is generally faster, cheaper, and considerably more private.

It's worth being clear about what a power of attorney does not do. It has nothing to do with what happens to your assets after you die — that's the job of the trust and the will discussed in the previous chapter. Its authority ends at death, at which point the trust you funded, or the applicable estate process for whatever was left outside it, takes over. A trust and a power of attorney cover different territory and different periods of your life. A comprehensive plan often uses both because each addresses a situation the other does not.

Choosing an agent matters as much as having the document. The most reliable agents tend to share three qualities: they're organized enough to manage paperwork under pressure, willing to actually act rather than freeze, and practically positioned to do so quickly when it counts. Many people name a spouse first and an adult child or sibling as a backup, in case the first choice is unavailable, incapacitated at the same time, or no longer living. Naming at least one successor is worth the extra sentence — the whole plan depends on someone being both willing and able when the moment arrives, and that someone isn't guaranteed to be your first choice.

One more trigger worth naming specifically: divorce. California automatically revokes a former spouse's designation as your power of attorney agent once the divorce is final. That sounds like good news, and mostly it is — but automatic revocation can also leave you without any agent at all if you never named a successor, or shift the role to a backup you chose years ago and might not choose today. Divorce should prompt an actual look at this document, not a quiet trust that the law already handled it.

By the time Frank recovered enough to sign documents himself, six weeks had passed, a conservatorship petition was partway through the courts, and Carol had spent several thousand dollars in legal fees to gain, temporarily, exactly the authority a properly signed piece of paper would have given her on day one. She withdrew the petition once Frank could sign for himself again. The first thing they did together afterward was execute powers of attorney for each other, sitting side by side at the same notary's office where they'd signed their mortgage papers decades earlier, naming their oldest daughter as the successor for both.

Is Your Power of Attorney Actually Ready?

- Do you have a durable power of attorney — one that explicitly states it survives incapacity — or only an informal document that may not meet current requirements?
- Have you given your named agent an actual copy, or does it exist only in a drawer they don't know about?
- Has a bank or financial institution seen the document in advance, or would your agent be presenting it for the first time in the middle of a crisis?
- Is a successor agent named, in case your first choice is unavailable when it matters?
- If you're married, does your spouse have one naming you, just as you have one naming them?

Reflection

If Carol's Tuesday happened to you tomorrow, does the person you'd want managing things actually have the legal authority to do it today — or only your assumption that they would?

The Difficult Question

Who would you actually want making decisions about your money if you couldn't speak for yourself, and have you ever told them that directly, in those words, rather than assuming they already know?

Chapter 4 — Your Voice in the Room You're Not In

Sofia's father had strong opinions about almost everything, for as long as she could remember — where to eat, how to load a dishwasher, which of his three children was currently disappointing him. What he never once said, in seventy-one years, was what he'd want to happen if a doctor ever asked whether to put him on a ventilator.

So when a fall left him in the ICU, unable to speak, unable to sign anything, and unable to tell anyone what he wanted, Sofia and her two brothers found themselves in a hospital conference room, all three legally equal in the eyes of the doctors, and all three certain they knew their father best.

They didn't agree. Marco wanted every possible intervention tried. Sofia thought their father would have hated the idea of machines keeping him technically alive with no real chance of recovery. Their younger brother, Diego, mostly wanted someone else to decide, so it wouldn't be his fault either way. Nobody was wrong to feel what they felt. Nobody had actually been told what their father wanted. Three adult children who loved him were left guessing, in real time, in a conference room, about a decision none of them had the standing to make alone and none of them could bear to make together.

An advance health care directive does two things at once, and it's worth understanding both separately, because most people only think about the first. The first is naming a health care agent — someone with clear legal authority to make medical decisions on your behalf if you can't make them yourself. That solves exactly the problem Sofia and her brothers ran into: instead of three people with equal standing and no tiebreaker, there's one person the law and the hospital recognize as the decision-maker.

The second, and the one almost everyone skips, is stating your own wishes: the kinds of treatment you would or wouldn't want, how you feel about life support and pain management, and where you land on the tradeoff between length of life and quality of life. Naming an agent answers who decides. Writing down your wishes answers what they're actually deciding based on. A directive that only does the first still leaves your agent guessing — with legal authority, but no more actual information than Sofia and her brothers had in that conference room.

Without a named agent, California law first looks for someone you personally designated to a provider, then an agent under a health care directive, then a court-appointed conservator or guardian with medical authority — a real, ordered chain, but only if one of those actually exists. When none of them does, the hospital can choose an appropriate person from a pool of family and close relationships instead: a spouse or partner, an adult child, a parent, a sibling, a grandchild, another relative, or even a close friend — chosen for having shown real care and involvement and for knowing the patient's values, not because of where their relationship falls on a list. There's no strict order among adult children, or among siblings, the way most people assume. When three adult children are all equally present and equally invested, as Sofia and her brothers were, nothing in the statute breaks the tie for them. That safety net exists for a reason, but it's not a substitute for naming your own agent — without one, the person the hospital lands on may not be the person you'd have chosen, and disagreement among people who all qualify can make an already hard moment considerably harder.

Most hospitals and providers are also bound by federal privacy law that limits what they can share, even with close family, without proper authorization. Naming a health care agent and having federal privacy law cooperate with that authority are related but not quite identical things. A well-drafted directive typically includes an explicit authorization for your agent to actually get information from your doctors, which is worth confirming rather than assuming one form automatically covers the other.

There's a second, related document worth knowing about, particularly for anyone already seriously ill or frail: a POLST, or Physician Orders for Life-Sustaining Treatment. Where an advance directive names an agent and states general wishes, a POLST is signed by a physician and functions as an actual medical order — the kind paramedics and hospital staff act on immediately, without needing to locate or interpret a longer document first. It doesn't replace a directive. It's a more specific, more urgent layer for people whose health has reached the point where someday has become soon.

The same kind of automatic protection that applies to other documents after a divorce applies here too: California revokes a former spouse's designation as your health care agent once the divorce is final. But automatic isn't the same as reviewed — revocation can leave you without any named agent at all, or shift the role to whoever you listed as a backup years earlier. A divorce is exactly the moment to look at this document again, not assume it already looked after itself.

Their father died eleven days later, after the three of them — with help from the hospital's palliative care team, who had clearly done this before — finally agreed on a direction none of them felt entirely at peace with, because none of them actually knew if it was the right one. What they inherited, along with the house and the modest savings he'd left behind, was a specific kind of guilt that doesn't show up on any balance sheet: the particular weight of having decided, without ever really knowing.

Sofia filled out her own advance health care directive four months later. She named her oldest daughter as her agent, named her younger daughter as the backup, and then did the part almost everyone skips: she sat both of them down at her own kitchen table — the same kind of table her father used to sit at, criticizing how she loaded the dishwasher — and actually told them what she wanted, out loud, in specific terms, more than once. Not because the document required it. Because she'd just spent eight months learning exactly what happens when nobody does.

Is Your Directive Actually Complete?

- Have you named a health care agent, and a backup in case your first choice is unavailable?
- Does the document authorize your agent to access your medical information, not just make decisions about it?
- Have you given copies to your agent, your backup, and your regular doctor — or does it only exist in a drawer?
- If you're seriously ill or frail, do you also have a POLST, or only a general directive?
- Have you actually told your agent what you want, in your own words, more than once?

Questions for Family Discussion

Not questions for a form. Questions for an actual conversation with the person you'd name as your agent:

- If there were only a small chance of meaningful recovery, would you want doctors to try everything anyway, or shift toward comfort?
- Is there a specific condition — permanent unconsciousness, no longer recognizing the people you love — where your answer changes?
- Who do you trust to interpret your wishes in a situation you never specifically discussed?
- Have you actually said any of this out loud, or only written it down?

Reflection

Think about the last time you talked with your family about how you'd want to be cared for — not in the abstract, but specifically. If you can't remember a time, that's not unusual. It does mean the person you'd name as your agent is currently guessing.

The Difficult Question

If your own children or siblings ended up in the room Sofia and her brothers were in, would they already know what you wanted — or would they be building their answer out of grief and guesswork, the way Sofia's family did, instead of anything you'd actually told them?

Chapter 5 — The Quiet Mistakes

Ruben had done real planning, and he had the folder to prove it — labeled in his own careful handwriting, updated twice in the decade before he died: once after he remarried, once after his second grandchild was born. Both times, he'd sat down with an attorney and made sure Marcus, his sister, and his wife Denise were named exactly as he intended.

What Ruben hadn't touched, because he never thought to, was a life insurance policy he'd bought in his twenties during his first marriage. The beneficiary form on file still named Elena — his first wife, Marcus's mother, whom he'd divorced amicably thirty-one years earlier and hadn't spoken to in over a decade.

When Ruben died, the policy — maintained for decades and worth just over two hundred thousand dollars — paid Elena. Not Denise. Not Marcus or his sister. The trust said nothing about it, because the trust never had any say in the policy's beneficiary designation.

This is, in its own quiet way, more common and more consequential than most people realize, and it happens for a completely understandable reason: a trust feels like the master document, the place where everything gets decided, so it's easy to assume it governs anything with your name on it. It doesn't.

Retirement accounts, life insurance policies, and many bank and brokerage accounts set up with a payable-on-death designation don't pass through your trust or your will at all. They pass by contract, directly, to whoever is named on the beneficiary form on file with the account itself — a separate instruction that lives with the bank, the insurance company, or the plan administrator, not with your attorney. The moment you die, that form generally controls, regardless of what your trust says, regardless of how recently you updated it, regardless of what you clearly would have wanted by then. Nobody checks the two documents against each other for you. Nobody is required to.

> ***California Law Note:*** *California's community property rules add another layer here, separate from federal law. Money earned or saved during a marriage often belongs to both spouses under California law, regardless of whose name is on a beneficiary form — the form controls who receives the funds, but community property rules can still affect who actually owned them to begin with. Employer retirement plans and IRAs don't always follow the same rules, either. Some plans require a spouse's written consent before someone else can be named to receive certain benefits, and that federal rule can override state law entirely; IRAs generally work differently. Because the rules vary this much, each account needs to*

be checked individually — the plan documents, the current beneficiary form, and, after a divorce, any court order addressing it — not assumed to work like the others.

The most common version of this mistake follows a predictable shape: a divorce, a remarriage, a new child, and an old account or policy that simply never gets revisited, because updating a trust feels like the whole job, and a beneficiary form feels like paperwork that was already handled years ago.

A related version is naming a minor child directly as a beneficiary, which creates its own complication: minors generally can't receive or manage a large sum directly, so the funds typically end up under a court-supervised arrangement until the child reaches adulthood — at which point they receive the full amount at once, with no staged distribution and no trustee's judgment involved, regardless of whether an eighteen-year-old is who you'd have chosen to hand that much money to all at once. Naming an appropriate trust for a minor's benefit, rather than the child directly, can avoid that court-supervised default — but retirement accounts specifically need their own tax analysis before naming a trust as beneficiary, since the rules for how quickly a trust has to draw down an inherited retirement account can be less forgiving than naming a person directly. This is exactly the kind of decision that needs a coordinated look from an attorney and a tax professional together, not a blanket rule applied to every account the same way.

Anything that isn't covered by a valid beneficiary designation and isn't titled in your trust falls back to exactly the process discussed three chapters ago: probate. This is the other half of the coordination problem — not just outdated forms overriding your intent, but forgotten assets that were never brought into either system at all, quietly defaulting into the slowest, most public, most expensive path available, simply because nobody checked.

Real estate adds one more layer worth naming specifically: property in another state, or another country, that isn't held in your trust generally requires its own separate proceeding — called ancillary probate — in the place where the property actually sits, even if your main estate is otherwise handled cleanly through your trust or through probate where you live. For property inside the United States, this typically means a second, smaller probate case in that other state. For property outside the United States, the equivalent process depends entirely on that country's own laws, and, as with the trust question in an earlier chapter, needs a conversation with an attorney who knows that specific jurisdiction, not a general answer here.

Marcus couldn't undo what had happened with his father's policy — the check to Elena had already been sent by the time anyone noticed, and there was no legal argument that changed what the form said. What he could do was go home and actually check his own. He logged into an account he hadn't looked at since the day he opened it and found two problems: an old 401(k) from a job he'd left nine years earlier, still listing a girlfriend he hadn't spoken to since, and a life insurance policy through his current employer that, it turned out, had no beneficiary named on it at all. Every policy has its own built-in default for exactly this situation, spelled out in the contract itself — some name the estate directly, others name a specific order of relatives first — and Marcus's policy happened to default straight to his estate, which meant, had anything happened to him, it would have gone through probate, the exact outcome his own trust was supposed to prevent.

Do Your Documents Actually Agree?

- Pull the actual beneficiary designation for every retirement account, life insurance policy, and payable-on-death account you own — not from memory, from the current form itself.
- Does each one match who you'd name today, or does it still reflect a relationship that's since changed?
- Is a minor ever named directly, rather than your trust or a trust created for their benefit?
- Is every account you own named somewhere — in a beneficiary designation or in your trust — or could something default into probate simply because nobody assigned it anywhere?
- If you own property in another state or country, has that been addressed separately from your primary plan?

Reflection

Most people can name their trust and their will without hesitating. Far fewer could tell you, without looking, exactly who's named on every retirement account and insurance policy they own. That gap is exactly where this chapter's mistakes live.

The Difficult Question

If you died today, is there an account or policy that would go to someone you haven't spoken to in years, simply because nobody ever went back and checked?

Part Three: The Pressures

Chapter 6 — When Family and Money Meet

Tomás and his brother Iván had never had a real fight in their lives—at least not one that lasted more than a day. That changed eleven months after Tomás received the proceeds of a settlement arising from the occupational lung disease he had developed after years of work. By then, he needed supplemental oxygen for much of the day, but he was still the person his family turned to whenever something went wrong. So when Iván asked to borrow eighteen thousand dollars to keep his auto repair shop open through a slow winter, Tomás agreed without giving it a second thought.

They put nothing in writing. Iván said he would repay the money within a year, and Tomás told him not to worry about it. They both understood that those words meant something, although they later disagreed about exactly what. They discussed neither interest nor payment terms and signed no document—just two brothers who loved each other, one helping the other in the most natural way he knew.

A year later, the shop was still struggling. Iván had repaid four thousand dollars in cash, a little at a time and always with an apology. Tomás never demanded the balance, but he never stopped noticing its absence. By the following Thanksgiving, the brothers treated each other with an excessive, almost ritual politeness. Tomás's portable oxygen concentrator rested beside his chair, so thoroughly integrated into the family's routine that no one paid attention to it anymore. Their mother could not identify what had changed between her sons, but everyone at the table could feel it.

Myth: *Saying no to a family member who asks for money is what damages the relationship.*

Reality: *More relationships are damaged by ambiguity than by an honest no. A clear answer, even a difficult one, respects the other person enough to give them something real to work with. A yes with no terms, or a maybe that drags on for months, usually costs more in the end than a clean, honest no ever would.*

What happened between Tomás and Iván wasn't really about the eighteen thousand dollars, and it wasn't really about whether Iván was a good or bad brother for asking, or whether Tomás was generous or foolish for saying yes. It was about the absence of a shared understanding of what, exactly, had been agreed to — which meant every silence afterward could be read as suspicion, or guilt, or resentment, depending on which of them was doing the reading that day.

This is the part almost nobody wants to hear: the single most protective thing you can do for a family loan isn't setting a harder boundary or saying no more often. It's writing the terms down, every time, even when it feels unnecessary, even when it feels like putting a business transaction on top of a family relationship that shouldn't need one.

A simple promissory note — a short document stating the amount, whether it's a loan or a gift, a repayment schedule if there is one, and whether interest applies — does something a handshake can't: it removes the guessing. It's not a sign of distrust. It's closer to the opposite. It's the thing that lets both people relax into the relationship instead of quietly keeping score of a debt nobody agreed on the terms of.

There's also a tax reason interest matters, beyond just clarity: an interest-free or below-market loan can carry its own tax consequences. A loan like theirs may be affected, and the interest rate and how it's documented are worth reviewing with a tax professional when the note is written, not after.

Part of what made Tomás and Iván's situation harder than it needed to be was that neither of them had actually decided, out loud, whether this was a loan or a gift. If you're going to give money to family and you don't really expect to see it again, saying so plainly — calling it a gift, not a loan — is kinder than a loan neither of you ever really intended to enforce. A gift with no strings attached and a clean conscience is a different thing entirely from a loan quietly rebranded as a gift by two people too uncomfortable to have the actual conversation.

Larger gifts can also carry tax reporting implications worth knowing about, even though for most families they don't result in an actual tax bill. As of 2026, an individual can generally give up to $19,000 to any one person without triggering a filing requirement, though certain situations — gift-splitting between spouses, a gift of a future interest rather than immediate use, and a handful of other specific circumstances — can require filing a return even within that amount. A married couple can generally combine their exclusions and give up to $38,000 to the same person, though splitting gifts this way requires filing a return to document it. Giving more than the exclusion doesn't usually trigger an immediate tax bill either — it requires filing IRS Form 709, and the excess simply counts against a much larger lifetime exclusion, currently $15 million per person. These figures move over time and should always be reconfirmed before a substantial gift is actually made.

The same principle extends to friends, arguably with even less room for error. Family relationships often have decades of history and something close to unconditional love to absorb some ambiguity; friendships, however close, usually don't have quite the same cushion. An undocumented loan to a friend that goes sideways doesn't just create tension — it can end the friendship outright, precisely because there's no assumed permanence forcing everyone back to the table at the next holiday. The same short document that protects a family relationship protects a friendship even more, because it's carrying more of the weight alone.

It took Tomás's wife, not Tomás, to finally name what was happening out loud. She caught him staring at his phone one night, Iván's name on the screen, a call not made again, and asked him, plainly, what exactly he thought the silence was protecting. She pointed out that it was costing them both more than eighteen thousand dollars ever could. Tomás called Iván the next week, not to ask for the money back, but to actually talk about it for the first time since the day he'd handed it over. They agreed, together, on what it actually was: six thousand dollars as a gift, outright, no further discussion needed, and twelve thousand as a loan with an actual schedule — two hundred dollars a month, no interest, written down this time, in an email both of them could point back to if either of them forgot. The specific terms mattered less than the fact that they'd finally agreed on what the terms were.

Before Money Changes Hands With Family or Friends

- Have you actually decided, out loud, whether this is a loan or a gift — not left it ambiguous for both of you to interpret differently later?
- If it's a loan, is there a written record of the amount, the schedule, and whether interest applies — even something as simple as an email both people can point back to?
- Have you thought about what you'll actually do if it isn't repaid, before you're in the middle of finding out?
- Are you saying yes because you want to, or because saying no feels unbearable in the moment — and would a clear no, kindly delivered, actually protect the relationship more than an ambiguous yes?

Reflection

Think of a time money moved between you and someone you love without any real conversation about what it meant. Where did the ambiguity end up living — in a document, or in a silence at the next family gathering?

The Difficult Question

If you said yes to every family request the way you have been, would you actually be able to keep saying yes indefinitely — and if not, does the person on the other end know that, or are they operating on an assumption you've never corrected?

Chapter 7 — Recognizing the Predators

Gloria had been a nurse for thirty-six years, the kind of career that teaches you to read people quickly and trust your own judgment. She'd raised two kids on that salary, paid off her house, and built a retirement account she was, reasonably, proud of. She was not an easy person to fool.

She met Derek at a "retirement planning" seminar at her church, the kind advertised with a free lunch. He wasn't pushy. He didn't ask for anything for months. He called to check in, remembered details about her grandchildren, seemed to genuinely enjoy their conversations about her late husband. By the time he mentioned an investment opportunity — a private fund, he said, that had returned eleven percent annually for six years running, guaranteed, available only to a small group of clients he handled personally — Gloria had known him for the better part of a year, and trusted him roughly as much as she trusted her own doctor.

> ***Myth:*** *People who fall for scams are careless or unintelligent.*
>
> ***Reality:*** *The most effective schemes are built specifically to work on careful, intelligent people, because those are the people with money worth targeting, and the ones an obviously rushed or clumsy pitch would never fool. Patience, warmth, and genuine-seeming rapport aren't signs something is safe. Often, they're signs someone has done their homework.*

A handful of patterns show up in almost every version of this, whether the pitch involves a stranger, a new friend, or someone from inside a trusted community.

Guaranteed returns are the single most reliable warning sign in investing. Every legitimate investment carries real risk, which means every investment's return is genuinely uncertain. Anyone promising a guaranteed high return, especially one that sounds only modestly better than the market rather than absurdly so, is either lying or doesn't understand what they're selling. Neither is someone you want managing your money.

Urgency and exclusivity do a scammer's work for them. "This has to happen today" and "this is only available to a small group" are both designed to short-circuit the one thing that protects almost everyone: time to think, and someone else to ask.

A request for secrecy is itself a red flag, not a sign of exclusivity. Legitimate professionals generally welcome a second opinion, because they have nothing to hide from one. Anyone who discourages you from mentioning an opportunity to your family, your accountant, or your attorney is telling you, directly, that the opportunity can't survive scrutiny.

A related pattern worth naming specifically: many of the most effective schemes work through communities built on trust — a church, a cultural or professional association, a tight-knit neighborhood — because a shared bond does a scammer's work for them, lending credibility an outsider would have to earn the hard way. The strength of a community is exactly what a predator borrows.

Gloria almost said yes on the spot. What stopped her wasn't suspicion — by that point, she genuinely liked Derek, and had no particular reason to doubt him. What stopped her was a rule she'd set for herself fifteen years earlier, after a different, smaller mistake: she never moved money without running it by her son first, no exceptions, no matter how good the idea sounded or how much she trusted the person proposing it.

Her son didn't know Derek, and had no particular reason to doubt him either. He asked exactly one question that mattered: could Derek provide his firm's registration number with state or federal securities regulators, the kind any legitimate investment professional can produce in about thirty seconds, and that anyone can independently verify through a public tool like FINRA's BrokerCheck, without relying on paperwork the person themselves provides. Derek could not. He had reasons — he was between firms, the fund was structured differently, he'd get her the paperwork soon — and every explanation was reasonable-sounding on its own and, together, added up to nothing.

This kind of exposure matters most, and comes looking hardest, in exactly the moments this book is about: a settlement, a business sale, an inheritance, a retirement account finally within reach. These moments are sometimes discoverable — through public court records, local news, or simply word getting around a small community — and they attract exactly the kind of attention Derek paid Gloria for the better part of a year. Being more careful right after a major liquidity event isn't paranoia. It's timing.

> ***California Law Note:*** *California has specific legal protections for the financial abuse of elders and dependent adults, broader than ordinary fraud law — covering far more than obvious theft, with remedies that can go beyond what an ordinary fraud claim allows.*

A related, quieter pattern is worth naming separately from a one-time pitch: financial exploitation by someone already inside the circle of trust — a caregiver, a new companion, sometimes even a family member — who doesn't propose a single opportunity but instead gradually takes over decisions, accounts, and access, one small step at a time, until the person being "helped" has lost track of how much control they've actually given up. This pattern rarely looks like fraud from the inside. It looks like someone being generous and helpful, right up until it doesn't. It's also a real argument for choosing a power of attorney agent carefully, discussed four chapters ago — the same authority that protects you in the right hands is exactly what this pattern exploits in the wrong ones.

Derek never did produce the paperwork. Gloria never invested, never heard from him again after a final, increasingly evasive phone call, and to this day doesn't know whether the fund was an outright fraud or simply an unlicensed, high-risk scheme dressed up to look safer than it was. What she does know is that the one habit she'd built fifteen years earlier — never deciding alone — had just protected six figures of retirement savings from a man she'd genuinely liked, for nearly a year, right up until the one question he couldn't answer.

Before You Trust the Opportunity

- Can the person offering this immediately provide verifiable registration or licensing — not a business card, an actual, independently checkable record?
- Does any part of the pitch involve secrecy, urgency, or discouraging you from getting a second opinion?
- Are the returns described as guaranteed, unusually high, or both — the two most reliable warning signs in combination?
- Have you verified this independently, through a source you found yourself, rather than one they provided?
- If a settlement, sale, or inheritance has recently become public or semi-public, are you being more careful right now, not less, since this is exactly when you're most likely to be targeted?

Reflection

Think about how you'd actually feel if a friend told you, gently, that they were worried about a financial decision you were making. Would you be able to hear it, or would you feel defensive? The people most vulnerable to sophisticated fraud are often the ones who've stopped letting anyone else weigh in.

The Difficult Question

If someone you trusted completely turned out to be wrong about something this important, would you find out from your own precautions — or only after the money was already gone?

Chapter 8 — When Relationships Change

Patricia and her ex-husband Greg built their landscaping company together, from a single truck and a client list of eleven houses to a business with twenty-two employees and a small fleet, over fifteen years of marriage. When they divorced four years ago, the settlement was, by their own account, more amicable than most: Patricia kept the business outright, Greg kept the house and most of their savings, and both of them told anyone who asked that they'd managed to end the marriage without destroying the friendship.

What the settlement handled cleanly on paper didn't automatically carry through everywhere else. In the months right after the divorce, while things between them were still genuinely friendly, Patricia had a new individual trust drafted to hold her now-sole ownership of the business — and when it came time to name a successor trustee, Greg felt like the obvious choice. He knew the business as well as anyone alive, and at the time, there was no one she trusted more with it.

That made sense four years ago. It made less sense with each year that passed, as the business grew into something considerably larger than what Greg had helped build, and as the two of them settled into something closer to old colleagues than the partnership that had made naming him feel natural in the first place. Nobody ever sat down and decided he should stop being her successor trustee. The choice from four years earlier just kept standing, because nothing had ever forced anyone to look at it again.

This is the part almost nobody expects: a choice that was completely reasonable when you made it doesn't come with an expiration date, or a reminder to reconsider it. Divorce itself doesn't erase an old decision — only a deliberate second look does, and deliberate second looks require someone to actually go back and take one.

California does provide some automatic protection here. Once a divorce is final, certain provisions in a will that benefit a former spouse are automatically revoked, unless the will specifically says otherwise — including gifts to that spouse and any nomination of them as executor, trustee, or in another fiduciary role. The will is then read as though the former spouse had already passed away.

A legal separation that doesn't end the marriage doesn't trigger this. Only an actual divorce or annulment does.

California automatically revokes a few other specific roles too: a former spouse named as your financial power of attorney agent, or as your health care agent under an advance directive, is removed from those roles the moment the divorce is final, by the same kind of automatic operation of law. But automatic doesn't mean confirmed — nobody sends a notice when it happens, and the only way to actually know your paperwork reflects it is to look.

California extends a similar kind of automatic revocation to some nonprobate transfers, but not uniformly, and this is where Patricia's second gap lived. She'd bought a modest personal life insurance policy years before the divorce, back when she and Greg first started the business together and wanted some ordinary protection in place for each other. The policy was entirely hers — her coverage, her premiums, nothing tied to the business itself — and Greg had simply been the obvious beneficiary to name at the time. After the divorce, updating it wasn't the kind of thing that came up. Life insurance beneficiary designations generally aren't reached by California's automatic nonprobate-transfer revocation, so a policy like Patricia's would ordinarily still pay as written unless the designation was changed or another controlling policy term or court order applied. Many employer-sponsored retirement plans present a different problem: federal rules may override state revocation law, and the plan may have to follow its own beneficiary records unless the participant changes them through the plan's procedures or a qualifying order applies. Courts have enforced plan documents even when the surrounding divorce paperwork appeared to point elsewhere.

Patricia's situation, then, was really two different versions of the same problem. The successor trustee choice wasn't ever wrong — it was right, once, and then simply never revisited as the reasons behind it quietly stopped applying. The life insurance was a different kind of gap entirely: a policy nobody had thought about in years, sitting exactly where it had been left, protected by exactly the kind of legal default that makes "the divorce probably handled it" such a dangerous assumption.

The safest rule is simple, given how unevenly the automatic protections actually reach: never rely on the divorce itself to update your plan. Review and replace, specifically, your trust, your will, your powers of attorney, your health care directive, your life insurance beneficiary, your retirement account beneficiary, and every role you'd assigned to your former spouse, once the divorce is final.

> ***Attorney's Perspective:*** *I ask every divorced client the same question: did you personally update your trust, your powers of attorney, and every beneficiary designation after the divorce — not assumed, personally confirmed? Many people assume the judgment took care of all of it. The law does revoke some things automatically. It doesn't safely or consistently redesign the whole plan, and guessing which parts it caught is a bad way to find out.*

Patricia caught both gaps only because a new attorney, helping her update her estate plan after a strong year for the business, asked to see everything she had rather than simply drafting something new — the trust's successor trustee line, and the life insurance policy neither of them had thought about in years. Greg, when she called to explain, wasn't offended — if anything, he seemed relieved, since he'd never actually wanted the responsibility and had simply never thought to bring it up either. Patricia named her sister as successor trustee, updated the life insurance beneficiary to reflect her own estate plan, and sent Greg a short, warm text thanking him for not making it complicated. He wrote back that he was glad someone had finally noticed.

After the Divorce Is Final

- Have you reviewed your trust specifically for any role — trustee, successor trustee, agent — still held by your former spouse, not just how assets are distributed?
- Have you checked the actual beneficiary designation on every retirement account and life insurance policy, since these may not update automatically even when other documents do?
- Have you personally confirmed — not assumed — what happened to any powers of attorney and health care directives that named your former spouse, since these revoke automatically but nobody sends a notice when it happens?
- If your divorce involved a business, does your succession plan for it still make sense under its current ownership, not its ownership at the time you first planned?
- Have you confirmed these changes with the institutions involved — the bank, the plan administrator — rather than assuming the paperwork updates itself?

Reflection

If you're divorced, or your marriage is ending, think about how long it's actually been since anyone looked at your full set of planning documents with fresh eyes. If the honest answer is since before the divorce, that's not unusual — but it does mean someone you no longer choose may still hold real authority over your affairs.

The Difficult Question

If something happened to you tomorrow, is there a chance a former spouse — not a current partner, not the people you'd choose today — would still have legal authority or a financial benefit you never meant to leave in place?

Part Four: Protecting What's Been Built

Chapter 9 — Lawsuits, Liability, and the Role of Insurance

Victor had spent nine years building his cleaning company from a single contract to a business with fourteen employees and steady revenue, and along the way, he'd bought a modest house and built up real savings. None of that had anything to do with the rainy Tuesday afternoon he glanced at a text message for two seconds too long and rear-ended a car stopped at a light, injuring the driver badly enough to require two surgeries and months of physical therapy.

Victor's auto policy — the same one he'd had since he was twenty-six, updated over the years only for the cars themselves, never for the coverage limits — capped out at a hundred thousand dollars in liability coverage. The other driver's medical bills alone came to nearly three hundred thousand dollars, before accounting for lost wages, pain and suffering, or anything else a court might eventually award.

This is where liability actually comes from, more often than people expect: not from owning a business, not from being careless or unlucky in any unusual way, but from ordinary moments — a car accident, a slip on a wet floor, a dog that's never bitten anyone until it does — that happen to collide with assets worth pursuing. The lawsuit doesn't care how the money was built. It only cares that it exists.

> ***Myth:*** *Assets held in a living trust are protected from lawsuits.*
>
> ***Reality: A revocable living trust — the kind discussed earlier in this book — generally provides no protection from your own creditors or a judgment against you during your lifetime. Because you can revoke it and reclaim the assets at any time, the law generally treats trust assets as still belonging to you for these purposes. A funded trust can avoid probate for the assets it governs and provide a private mechanism for incapacity. It was never built to protect those assets from your own judgment creditors, and believing otherwise is one of the more expensive misunderstandings in this entire book.***

Standard auto and home insurance policies are built for ordinary risk, with limits that made sense for most people's finances at some point and haven't necessarily kept pace with anyone's actual net worth since. An umbrella policy sits on top of those standard policies and extends liability coverage well beyond their limits, often into the millions, and often costs far less than most people expect relative to the protection it adds.

For business owners specifically, the business itself is worth structuring properly — an LLC or corporation, maintained the way the law expects it to be, so that a claim against the business doesn't automatically reach personal assets, and a claim against you personally doesn't automatically reach the business. That structure protects a different kind of exposure than insurance does, and neither one substitutes for the other. Victor's accident had nothing to do with his business, and his business's liability structure, however well maintained, would have done nothing to protect his house from what happened that Tuesday.

One important caution: none of this works retroactively. Moving assets into an LLC, gifting them to family, or restructuring ownership specifically to keep them away from a claim that's already arisen — or one you can see coming — can be challenged and unwound by a court. It isn't automatic, but it's a real risk, and it can leave you worse off than doing nothing at all. Asset protection has to happen before trouble arrives, not in reaction to it.

California also provides a homestead exemption that protects a portion of the equity in your primary home from certain creditors trying to force a sale to satisfy a judgment. The protected amount isn't a fixed number — it's generally tied to the median home price in your county from the prior year, within a statutory floor and ceiling that get adjusted over time. It's worth understanding what this exemption doesn't do: it doesn't erase your mortgage, and it doesn't stop your own mortgage lender from foreclosing if you fall behind on payments. What it does is limit how much of your home's protected equity a qualifying creditor can actually reach.

Victor's case settled within his policy limits, but only because his attorney negotiated hard and got fortunate — the other driver's injuries, serious as they were, ultimately settled for less than a jury might have awarded had it gone to trial. Victor didn't wait to see whether he'd get fortunate a second time. He called his insurance agent the next week — a woman he'd been paying for eleven years and had spoken to maybe three times — added a million-dollar umbrella policy for less than the cost of his cell phone bill, and finally told her, for the first time in nine years, what his business actually looked like now.

The Five-Minute Version

- Review your auto and home insurance liability limits on purpose, at least once a year — not just when the premium happens to change.
- Review umbrella coverage in light of your current assets, income, activities, and liability risks — not the financial picture you had when you first bought the policy.
- Confirm your business is actually structured and maintained the way the law expects, not just filed once and forgotten.
- Remember what your trust doesn't do: it offers no protection from your own creditors during your lifetime.
- Tell your insurance agent what's actually changed in your finances recently. They can't protect what they don't know about.

Reflection

Think about the last ordinary moment — a distracted second, a wet floor, an unleashed dog — that could have gone differently. Insurance isn't about assuming the worst will happen. It's about making sure an ordinary moment doesn't cost you everything else you've built.

The Difficult Question

If the accident that happened to Victor happened to you tomorrow, would your insurance actually cover what a court might award, or would you find out, for the first time, exactly how much of what you've built was never actually protected?

Chapter 10 — Working With the Tax Landscape

Estela had spent thirty years as an accountant before she retired, which is exactly why the mistake surprised her as much as it did. She understood taxes. She'd just never thought to mention, to the financial advisor recommending she convert eighty thousand dollars from her traditional IRA to a Roth IRA that year, that her mother had also died that spring, and that inherited stock had risen sharply between its date-of-death valuation and the day Estela sold it.

Neither decision was wrong on its own. Converting to a Roth IRA before required distributions push you into a higher bracket later is a genuinely sound strategy, and selling inherited stock — usually with little or no capital gains tax owed, for reasons discussed below — is often the right call too. What nobody caught was that doing both in the same year stacked two separate sources of income on top of each other, pushing Estela into a considerably higher tax bracket than either decision would have triggered alone. Her financial advisor didn't know about the inheritance. Her tax preparer didn't find out about either decision until the following spring, filing a return for a year that had already happened.

> ***Myth:*** *If I have significant assets, my family will owe estate tax when I die.*
>
> ***Reality:*** *The federal estate tax exemption is high enough that the large majority of American families, even genuinely wealthy ones, never actually owe it. The tax most people actually need to plan around isn't estate tax. It's income and capital gains tax, which work completely differently and apply to nearly everyone.*

One mechanism worth understanding on its own, because it quietly protects more families than almost anything else in this book: when you inherit an appreciated asset — a house, stock, most other investments — its cost basis for tax purposes generally resets to its value on the date the person who owned it died, rather than what they originally paid for it. This is called a step-up in basis, and it means the appreciation that happened during their lifetime is usually never taxed as a capital gain to the person who inherits it. It's a large part of why Estela's stock sale created relatively little tax on its own — the gain that mattered, for tax purposes, was only the amount the stock had moved since her mother's death, not the decades of growth before it.

California, as a community property state, extends this further for married couples in a way separate-property states typically don't: when one spouse dies, property that genuinely qualifies as community property can receive a full step-up in basis on both halves, not just the half that belonged to the spouse who died. That word "qualifies" matters — simply having both spouses' names on a title doesn't automatically make something community property for tax purposes. It depends on how the asset was actually acquired and characterized, which is exactly why keeping records of how and when property was bought, and how it's titled, is worth doing now, not reconstructing later when it matters most.

It's also worth separating, clearly, three different taxes that tend to blur together in most people's minds. Income tax applies to what you earn, every year, regardless of what you're worth. Capital gains tax applies specifically to the growth in value of something you sell. Estate tax is different from both — a federal tax that, for deaths in 2026, applies only to estates above $15 million per person, an amount Congress sets and periodically changes, with married couples often able to combine both spouses' exemptions through a process called portability. That requires a timely federal filing, even when no estate tax is immediately due — worth raising promptly with a tax professional rather than assumed to happen on its own. California currently imposes no separate estate or inheritance tax, but an estate or trust may still have its own California income tax filing to handle, separate from what any individual beneficiary owes, if it earns income while it's being administered. Inheriting the asset itself isn't usually a taxable event. What you do with it afterward can be.

Retirement accounts add one more layer of coordination that's changed meaningfully in recent years: the rules governing how quickly a non-spouse beneficiary has to withdraw an inherited retirement account, and pay income tax on those withdrawals, have gotten considerably less generous than they used to be, and who you name as beneficiary — a person directly, or your trust — can change how those rules apply. This is exactly the kind of detail that goes stale fastest, and exactly why the answer belongs to whoever is currently doing your planning, not to a book.

Estela's advisor and her tax preparer had never spoken to each other, not once, in the six years she'd worked with both of them. She fixed that the following week, not by finding new professionals, but by putting the two people she already trusted directly in touch, one email, both of them copied, one line at the top: "From now on, you two talk before I do anything." It cost her nothing extra. It also meant the mistake never repeated itself.

Is Your Tax Picture Actually Coordinated?

- Do your attorney, your CPA or tax preparer, and your financial advisor actually know about each other, or are they each working from a partial picture of your finances?
- Before a significant financial decision — selling an asset, converting an account, taking a large distribution — has anyone checked what else is happening that same tax year?
- Do you know, roughly, whether your estate is anywhere near the federal estate tax exemption, or are you planning around a tax that likely doesn't apply to you while overlooking the ones that do?

- If you've inherited or expect to inherit appreciated assets, do you understand how the step-up in basis affects what you'd owe if you sold them?
- When did your plan last get reviewed specifically for tax law changes, rather than just major life events?

Reflection

Think about whether your attorney, your accountant, and your financial advisor have ever actually spoken to each other, about you, at the same time. If the honest answer is no, that's not unusual — but it does mean nobody currently has the full picture.

The Difficult Question

If you made a significant financial decision tomorrow, is there anyone in your life whose job it is to notice how it interacts with everything else — or is coordinating your own advisors, quietly, entirely on you?

Part Five: Complex Lives

Chapter 11 — Blended Families

Beatriz's father remarried when she was nine, two years after her mother died, and by every account, built a genuinely happy second marriage that lasted until his death twenty-six years later. He loved his second wife, Diane, completely, and he loved his three children from his first marriage exactly as much. When he did his estate planning, in his sixties, he did the thing that felt simplest and most trusting: he left everything to Diane outright, with the clear, sincere understanding — spoken between them many times, something close to "whatever's left goes to the kids, you know that" — that she would eventually leave a meaningful portion to Beatriz and her siblings.

Diane meant it, at the time. She also lived another nineteen years after Beatriz's father died, built a full life of her own during those years, grew genuinely close to her own grandchildren from a daughter she'd had before ever meeting Beatriz's father, and updated her estate plan twice along the way — each time, a little further from the family she'd married into decades earlier, and a little closer to the one she'd actually spent her final two decades with. When Diane died, her estate went entirely to her own daughter and grandchildren. Beatriz and her siblings received nothing, not because Diane broke a promise on purpose, but because the promise was never anything more than a promise, and nineteen years is a long time for a life, and a heart, to drift.

What happened to Beatriz's family is the single most common failure in blended-family planning, and it happens for a completely understandable reason: leaving everything outright to a spouse feels like the ultimate expression of trust, and it is — but trust isn't a legal mechanism. Once assets pass outright to a surviving spouse, that spouse owns them completely, with full legal authority to change their own estate plan however their life leads them to, at any point, for any reason, including no reason at all. A verbal promise, even a heartfelt one, made in a moment of genuine intention, has no legal weight nineteen years later against whatever document is actually signed at the end.

Myth: *My spouse will naturally take care of my kids from a prior marriage after I'm gone.*

Reality: *Good intentions aren't a legal mechanism. Once assets pass outright to a spouse, they're free to change their own estate plan however their life leads them to, at any point, for any reason. If you want your children guaranteed an inheritance regardless of what your spouse's life looks like decades from now, that guarantee has to be built into the structure itself, not left to a promise, however sincere.*

The structure built for exactly this situation is often called a marital trust, or sometimes a QTIP trust — the specific name matters less than what it does. It can provide fully for a surviving spouse during their lifetime — income, the right to live in the family home, support for ordinary needs — without ever giving them the power to redirect where what's left eventually goes. When the surviving spouse dies, the remaining assets pass to whoever the first spouse named from the start, regardless of what the surviving spouse might want by then, regardless of how much their own life has changed in the meantime.

This structure only works with property that's actually yours to direct: your separate property, and your own half of whatever was acquired during the marriage. It doesn't reach your spouse's half of community property — that remains theirs to leave however they choose, regardless of what your own plan says.

It's also worth being direct about something many people assume incorrectly: a stepchild ordinarily doesn't inherit from a stepparent under California's default intestacy rules merely because of the family relationship, even after decades together, unless a will or trust specifically includes them, or a formal adoption took place. California does recognize limited exceptions, but relying on one is not a plan. Love and a lived relationship don't create legal rights on their own. If you want a stepchild treated as your own child for inheritance purposes, that has to be written down specifically — it doesn't happen by default, no matter how long or how close the relationship.

Blended families sometimes span more than one household structure — they also span borders. A parent with children living in Mexico from an earlier relationship, or a stepparent whose own family remains there, faces the added layer discussed earlier in this book: a U.S. trust doesn't automatically extend its authority to property or family members abroad, and whether or how it can depends entirely on the laws of wherever they are. Providing for family members who live in another country, or who may need to receive an inheritance while living there, is worth a specific conversation with someone who understands both systems, not an assumption that the plan built here simply crosses the border with you.

Beatriz is remarried now, with two kids from her first marriage and a husband she genuinely loves. She didn't need anyone to explain to her why a simple outright gift to a spouse wasn't enough — she'd lived the alternative. Her own plan uses exactly the structure her father never did: her husband is fully provided for, for the rest of his life, and whatever remains afterward is already, legally, guaranteed to reach her own children. She told him why, over dinner, the week they signed everything — not because she doubted him, but because she'd watched what happens when even the people who mean it most only have a promise to stand on. Nobody's intentions have to survive an unknowable number of years of an unknowable future. The document already has.

Does Your Plan Actually Protect Everyone You Intend?

- If you're leaving assets outright to a spouse, have you talked honestly about what happens to those assets after they're gone — not what you hope happens, but what's legally guaranteed to happen?
- Are your stepchildren specifically named in your documents, or are you assuming a relationship creates a legal right it doesn't actually create?
- Have you considered a trust structure that provides for your spouse during their lifetime while still guaranteeing what remains reaches your own children?

- If your blended family spans more than one household — including family members living outside the country — has that been addressed specifically, not assumed to be covered by your main plan?
- Have you had an honest conversation with your spouse about this, even though it's uncomfortable, rather than leaving it to a verbal understanding only one of you may remember the same way?

Reflection

Think about what you actually know, versus what you assume, about what happens to your family's assets after both you and your spouse are gone. If the honest answer relies on trust rather than a document, that's worth naming clearly, at least to yourself.

The Difficult Question

If your spouse outlives you by twenty years and builds a life you can't currently imagine, would your children still inherit what you intend for them today — or only what your spouse still wants for them by then?

Chapter 12 — Planning for the Next Generation

Yolanda and David had done almost everything right. Two years after Yolanda's settlement came through, they'd found an attorney, set up a trust, retitled their house, updated their beneficiary forms — all of it, methodically, the way people do when they've decided to take something seriously. Then their attorney asked one question, and the whole process stalled for fourteen months: if something happened to both of you, who would raise Emma and Noah?

It wasn't that they didn't have candidates. It was that naming one meant, for just a moment, actually picturing the specific version of the future where both of them were gone and their four-year-old and seven-year-old needed somewhere to live. Every other document in their plan was about property. This one was about their children, sitting in a room, being told their parents weren't coming back. Neither of them could get through a conversation about it without one of them changing the subject.

This is, by a wide margin, the most commonly avoided piece of planning among parents of young children, and it happens for a reason that has nothing to do with carelessness: naming a guardian requires imagining the one scenario every parent works hardest not to imagine. Trusts and beneficiary forms are abstractions. This isn't.

But avoiding the decision doesn't remove it. It just moves it — from you, now, with full knowledge of your children and your family, to a judge, later, with none of it. Without a nominated guardian, a court decides who raises your children if both parents are gone, based on a hearing, possibly among family members who disagree with each other about who's best suited, at exactly the moment your children can least afford the disruption of that uncertainty.

> ***Attorney's Perspective:*** *The guardian nomination is almost always the last blank filled in on a new-parent estate plan, and sometimes the plan sits unfinished for months because of exactly this one line. I've learned not to rush it. I've also learned that most parents, once they finally have the conversation, describe it as far less painful than the year they spent avoiding it.*

Naming a guardian in your will doesn't remove the court's role — a judge still has to approve the appointment and remains guided by the child's best interests. But a parent's nomination gives the court clear evidence of the parent's wishes and can carry substantial weight, instead of leaving the choice to be reconstructed after a crisis.

The second decision — not who raises your children, but how they'd actually receive whatever you leave them — is a separate question, and an equally avoidable one. Leaving assets directly to a minor child creates exactly the complication mentioned earlier in this book: the funds typically end up under court supervision until the child turns eighteen, at which point they receive the entire amount at once, with no staged distribution and no adult judgment involved in how it's used.

A trust built specifically for a minor solves this differently. You choose the trustee — often, but not always, the same person raising the child — and you choose the terms: distributions for education and reasonable needs along the way, and the remainder released in stages, at ages you decide, rather than the whole amount landing on an eighteen-year-old the week they're legally an adult but not necessarily anywhere close to financially ready. Some parents stage it at twenty-five, thirty, and thirty-five. Some release it all at once, later. There's no universally right answer, only a decision that's actually yours to make, instead of a default nobody chose.

One situation deserves its own mention. If a child or other beneficiary receives SSI, Medicaid, or another means-tested benefit, an outright inheritance or an improperly designed trust can jeopardize their eligibility. Specialized planning — a special-needs trust, built for exactly this — can let family assets support that person without unintentionally replacing the benefits they depend on. This is worth raising directly with an attorney, not something to assume a standard trust structure already handles.

It's worth considering, deliberately, whether the guardian and the trustee should be the same person. Often they are, and that's a reasonable choice. But they don't have to be — someone might be the guardian you trust most with your children's daily life and upbringing, while someone else, equally trusted, might be better suited to managing money responsibly on their behalf. Separating the roles isn't a sign of distrust in either person. It's simply matching each responsibility to where it fits best.

What finally moved Yolanda and David wasn't a deadline or a lecture. It was Yolanda's sister asking, gently, over dinner, whether they'd figured out the guardian question yet — not pressuring, just asking, the way people who love you sometimes do. They finished the conversation that weekend. Yolanda's sister would be the guardian. For trustee, they didn't default to the same choice — they actually talked it through, and landed somewhere else: David's brother, steadier with a spreadsheet than a bedtime routine, willing to hold the money without needing to raise the kids too. They called both to ask if they'd actually be willing, got two yeses, and signed the amended documents within the month. Fourteen months of avoidance ended in about three days, once they let themselves actually have the conversation instead of circling it.

Questions for the Conversation You've Been Avoiding

Not questions to answer alone, checking boxes. Questions to actually ask each other, out loud — the conversation Yolanda and David spent fourteen months avoiding:

- If something happened to both of us, who would you want raising the kids — and is that actually the same person I'd choose?
- Have we asked that person directly, or are we just assuming they'd say yes?

- Should the same person handle the money and raise the kids day to day, or does that need to be two different people?
- If we're staging when the kids receive anything, what ages actually make sense to us — not a default, an actual answer?

Reflection

If the guardian conversation is the one piece of your plan you've been avoiding, notice that clearly, without judgment. It's the most commonly avoided decision in this entire book, for good reason. Naming it as avoidance, rather than as something you'll get to eventually, is usually what finally moves it forward.

The Difficult Question

If something happened to both you and your co-parent tomorrow, is there a real, current answer to where your children would go — or only a conversation you've been meaning to finish?

Chapter 13 — Passing On What You Built

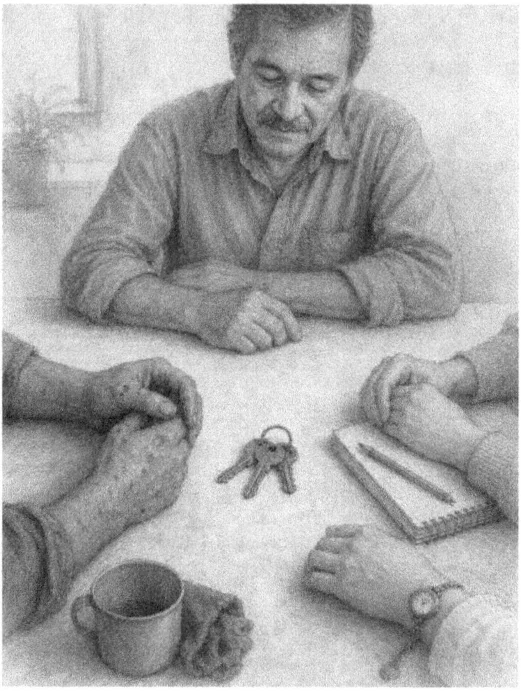

Fernando built his auto repair business from one bay in a rented garage to three locations over thirty-one years, and for most of that time, his plan for what happened to it after him was simple, and felt fair: split it three ways, equally, among his kids. Luis, Camila, and Rosa would each own a third.

It felt fair because it was equal. It took his attorney fifteen minutes to explain why it wasn't the same thing.

Luis had worked in the business since he was nineteen, currently ran two of the three locations, and had turned down other opportunities more than once specifically because he assumed he'd eventually run the whole thing. Camila taught high school math. Rosa was a nurse. Neither had ever changed the oil on a car in her life, and neither wanted to. Under Fernando's original plan, all three would inherit equal ownership, equal voting power, and an equal say in how a business two of them had never worked a day in was run — while Luis, who'd have to keep showing up every morning managing employees, payroll, and three locations, would have no more authority over any of it than his sisters, despite doing all the actual work.

> ***Myth:*** *Splitting a family business equally among all your children is the fairest way to pass it on.*
>
> ***Reality:*** *Equal ownership and equal involvement are different things, and treating them as the same usually satisfies nobody — not the child actually running the business without proportionate authority, and not the children who inherit a stake in something they have no interest in managing. Fair often means giving each child something appropriate to their actual relationship with the business, not identical shares of the same asset.*

This is the single most common structural mistake in family business succession, and it comes from conflating two genuinely different questions: who owns the business, and who runs it. Equal ownership sounds fair because it treats children the same. But running a business and owning a passive share in one are entirely different relationships to it, and defaulting to identical treatment for both usually satisfies neither the child doing the work nor the children who aren't.

A more deliberate approach separates the two questions on purpose. Luis, doing the actual work, can receive controlling ownership, or a structure that gives him real operational authority — voting shares, or a management role formalized in the business's own governing documents — regardless of what percentage of the underlying value he owns. Camila and Rosa can still inherit meaningful economic value from the business, or its equivalent, without holding voting power over decisions they have neither the expertise nor the desire to make.

One common way to balance this: if the business is the largest asset in the estate, a life insurance policy sized to roughly match the value of the business can go to the children not receiving ownership, so everyone still receives comparable value — just not the same asset. Luis gets the business he's already running. Camila and Rosa get something they can actually use, rather than a fractional, illiquid stake in a business they'd have no real voice in and no interest in managing.

A related tool worth knowing about, particularly if the business might eventually be co-owned by more than one sibling: a buy-sell agreement, which sets out in advance what happens if an owner wants to leave, becomes unable to work, or dies — including how the business gets valued for that purpose, so a dispute over price doesn't become its own crisis on top of everything else.

Businesses with operations, suppliers, or ownership interests across the border into Mexico add a real layer of complexity to succession planning — different business registration systems, different tax treatment, sometimes different rules about foreign ownership of certain business types. If any part of what you've built operates or is owned across that line, the succession plan needs input from someone who understands both countries' business and tax law, not just an assumption that a U.S. succession plan automatically covers the whole operation.

Fernando told all three of his children together, on a Sunday, not because he needed their permission but because thirty-one years of saying "equal" out loud meant he owed them the same directness now that he was changing his mind. Camila's only question was whether Luis was doing okay running the shops alone most days. Neither sister mentioned the money.

Fernando's revised plan gave Luis controlling ownership of the business itself, formalized the role he was already doing in the company's own governing documents, and used a life insurance policy — sized to roughly match what a third of the business was worth — to leave Camila and Rosa each a comparable inheritance in cash, free and clear, with no obligation to the business at all. Luis still calls his sisters when something significant comes up, not because the documents require it, but because he wants to. That's a different thing than needing their vote.

Does Your Succession Plan Match Reality?

- If more than one child could inherit the business, have you separated who would actually run it from who would simply own a share?
- Does the child doing the work have real operational authority, or just an equal vote among people who don't do the work?
- If other children aren't receiving ownership, have you used another asset — like life insurance — to give them comparable value?
- Is there a buy-sell agreement or similar structure governing what happens if an owner leaves, becomes unable to work, or dies?
- If your business has any cross-border operations or ownership, has that been addressed by someone who understands both countries' business law?

Reflection

Think honestly about which of your children, if any, would actually want to run what you've built — not who you assume should, out of birth order or a sense of obligation, but who genuinely would.

The Difficult Question

If you split your business equally among your children today, would the ones actually doing the work feel like owners, or like employees with extra paperwork?

Part Six: Building and Sustaining the Plan

Chapter 14 — Assembling Your Professional Team

Antonio had inherited a small apartment building from his uncle eleven years earlier, held onto it through two decades of appreciation, and finally decided to sell it the year he turned sixty. Before he signed anything, he did something that took him about two weeks and changed almost nothing about the sale itself: he got his attorney, his CPA, his financial advisor, and his insurance agent on the same email thread.

The attorney flagged that the building was titled in Antonio's name, not his trust — a gap from years earlier that nobody had caught, and one that needed fixing before closing, not after. The CPA ran the numbers on timing: selling in

December instead of January, given what else was happening in Antonio's finances that year, saved him a meaningful amount by avoiding the same kind of bracket-stacking Estela ran into four chapters ago. The financial advisor flagged that the proceeds, once they landed, would push one of Antonio's accounts past a threshold worth reconsidering for a Roth conversion the following year — a decision none of the other two would have thought to raise, because it wasn't their area. And his insurance agent asked the one question nobody else on the thread would have thought to: whether his liability coverage had kept pace with what he was actually worth now — the same gap that had caught Victor unprepared five chapters back.

It's worth being clear about what each of these professionals actually does, since the roles blur together in most people's minds, and that blurring is part of why coordination breaks down.

An estate planning attorney builds and maintains the legal structure — the trust, the will, the powers of attorney, the health care directive — and understands how ownership, control, and legal authority actually work. A CPA or tax preparer understands the tax consequences of what you're doing, this year and going forward, and can catch exactly the kind of timing problem that cost Estela real money. A financial advisor manages the money itself — investments, retirement accounts, the broader financial picture — and thinks about your finances as a whole, moving system, not a single transaction. An insurance professional evaluates and structures the coverage that protects everything the other three are managing.

Each one is genuinely expert in their own area. None of them is positioned to see the whole picture alone, because none of their job descriptions include it.

Attorney's Perspective: *I've started asking new clients, directly, in the first meeting: who's your CPA, and would you mind if I reached out to them? Most people are surprised by the question. Almost all of them say yes. The ones who've had a bad surprise before usually wish someone had asked sooner.*

Nobody on that team is going to spontaneously call the other two, not because they're careless, but because coordinating with other professionals isn't part of what any of them are specifically hired or paid to do, and reaching out takes initiative nobody's specifically responsible for. The connection has to come from somewhere, and in practice, it almost always has to come from you — not because you're expected to understand tax law or trust law yourself, but because you're the only person in the relationship who's actually talking to all three.

This doesn't require anything elaborate. A shared email thread, the way Antonio used, works. So does simply asking each professional, directly, whether they've spoken with the others recently, and following up if the answer is no. Before any significant decision — selling something, converting an account, changing a business structure, receiving a large sum — a short conversation among your team, even a fifteen-minute call, is worth more than any individual piece of advice given in isolation.

The sale closed in December, exactly as the CPA recommended. The trust got amended before closing, exactly as the attorney caught. The umbrella policy got updated the same week, exactly as the insurance agent flagged. And the following spring, when Antonio and his financial advisor sat down to talk about the Roth conversion, the advisor already knew what the CPA had done the year before, because Antonio had kept them talking to each other the whole way through. Nothing about Antonio's plan was more sophisticated than anyone else's in this book. It was simply coordinated, on purpose, by someone who'd decided that was his job.

Is Your Team Actually a Team?

- Can you name your attorney, your CPA or tax preparer, your financial advisor, and your insurance professional — not just "I have someone for that," but an actual name for each?
- Do any two of them know the others exist, or does each one only know what you've personally told them?
- Before your last significant financial decision, did anyone on your team talk to anyone else on your team about it?
- If you don't have one of these four professionals yet, is that because you don't need one, or because you haven't gotten around to finding one?
- Would you know who to call first if something significant happened, or would you be figuring out your own team in the middle of the moment that needed it?

Reflection

Think about the last time two of your professional advisors actually spoke to each other, about you, without you being the one relaying information between them. If you can't think of a time, that's the gap this chapter is asking you to close.

The Difficult Question

If you disappeared tomorrow, would your team know enough about each other, and about your actual situation, to keep your family's plan working — or does all of the coordination currently exist only inside your own head?

Chapter 15 — The Plan That Outlives the Moment

Josefina signed her first trust at forty-five, the year she and her husband finally felt like their savings had become something worth protecting rather than just accumulating. She did everything right that day — funded it, named agents, had the conversation about guardianship for their youngest, still eleven at the time.

Then she did the thing almost nobody in this book managed to do the first time: she put a date on her calendar, five years out, to look at all of it again. Not because anything specific would change. Just because five years is a long time, and she'd learned, from a friend's situation years earlier, that the plans people never revisit are usually the ones that eventually fail them.

At fifty, the review turned up nothing dramatic — a beneficiary form on an old employer account that needed updating, a successor trustee whose contact information had changed. Small things. Fifteen minutes with her attorney to catch them.

At fifty-five, it turned up more: her younger daughter, the one who'd needed a guardian named at eleven, was now twenty-one, married, with a stepson of her own — a blended family forming one generation down from Josefina's own trust, needing exactly the kind of conversation covered several chapters earlier in this book. Josefina's own plan didn't need to change for that. But she made sure her daughter had the same conversation she'd had at forty-five, before her daughter needed it the way Josefina once had.

At sixty, the federal estate tax exemption had changed since her original plan was drafted — a detail her attorney tracked so she didn't have to, but one that would have made real parts of a decade-old plan out of date if nobody had been checking. At sixty-five, her husband had a health scare that resolved without lasting damage, but that made the incapacity provisions in both of their plans feel, for the first time, less theoretical than they had at forty-five.

None of these moments were emergencies. That was the point. Josefina's plan never had to survive a crisis it wasn't built for, because she kept checking whether it was still built for the life she was actually living.

Set it and forget it is the most common mistake in estate planning, more costly, in aggregate, than any single wrong decision, because it isn't one mistake — it's the thing that lets every other mistake in this book keep operating undetected. Renata's trust sat unfunded for three years because nobody checked. Ruben's beneficiary form sent two hundred thousand dollars to the wrong person because nobody checked. Patricia's ex-husband stayed named as successor trustee for four years after their divorce because nobody checked. None of these were failures of the underlying legal tools. Trusts work. Beneficiary designations work exactly as designed. The failure, every time, was treating a plan as something you finish once, rather than something you maintain.

Certain moments should trigger a review regardless of when the calendar says the next one is due: a birth, a death, a marriage, a divorce, buying or selling a significant asset, moving to a new state, a significant change in health, or a business changing hands. Any of these can make part of an existing plan wrong, not just outdated.

> ***Attorney's Perspective:*** *The clients whose plans actually hold up, years later, are rarely the ones who spent the most on their first draft. They're the ones who came back. A plan I never see again is a plan I can't help stay current, no matter how carefully it was built the first time.*

Josefina is seventy-one now. Her next review is on the calendar, eighteen months out, exactly as it has been every few years since she was forty-five. She has no particular reason to expect it will turn up anything dramatic. That has never actually been the point.

The Two Reasons to Open the File Again

There are really only two legitimate reasons to open your plan again, and everything else is either avoidance or noise.

The first is a trigger event: a birth, a death, a marriage, a divorce, a significant asset bought or sold, a move to a new state, a real change in health, a business changing hands. Any one of these can make part of an existing plan wrong, not just outdated, and any one of them is reason enough to look, regardless of when your last review happened to be.

The second is simpler, and easier to ignore: time itself. Even when nothing dramatic has happened, three to five years is long enough for the law to have shifted quietly underneath you, and for the plan itself to have quietly stopped matching the life you're actually living — who you'd choose today, not who you chose back then.

If you can't point to one of those two things — an actual event, or an actual date on a calendar — that's the answer already. It's time.

Reflection

Look back across every chapter in this book, and notice what's actually common to all of them. It was never really about the trust, or the power of attorney, or the beneficiary form. It was about a decision, made once, that then had to survive contact with an actual, changing life. The plan that survives isn't the one that was drafted most carefully. It's the one somebody kept coming back to.

The Difficult Question

The moment that brought you to this book — the settlement, the sale, the inheritance, the decades of saving — was one decision. Is the plan you build from here going to be one decision too, or an ongoing one?

Epilogue — Stewardship, Not Fear

Maria's kitchen is different now. Not the room itself — the same table, the same window over the sink, the same chipped mug in the drying rack most mornings — but what happens in it. Eleven months after she stood there holding her mother's coffee mug, unable to think of a single next step, she sat at that same table with her own two kids, seventeen and twenty, and told them, plainly, what she'd learned: where the important papers were, who to call, what she wanted if something ever happened to her the way it had happened to her mother. Her son asked if this meant something was wrong. She told him no. It meant the opposite.

None of what's in this book was ever really about the documents. A trust is a container. A power of attorney is a permission slip for a version of you that can't currently speak for itself. A beneficiary form is an instruction, quietly filed, that will one day matter more than almost anything else you've ever signed. Every one of them is powerless without the decision underneath it — the actual, specific, sometimes uncomfortable choice about who you trust, what you owe, and what you want to happen to the people and things you've spent a lifetime building, long after you're no longer the one managing any of it.

That decision was never going to arrive by accident. It had to be made, on purpose, by someone willing to sit with questions most people spend a lifetime avoiding: who raises your children if you can't. Who speaks for you if you're unable to speak for yourself. What happens to a business, or a house, or a retirement account built over forty quiet years, once the family that exists ten years from now looks nothing like the one that exists today.

You didn't pick up this book because you wanted more paperwork. You picked it up, whatever door you came through, because something had changed enough to make the paperwork feel urgent — and what you actually needed, underneath that urgency, was never a document. It was a strategy: a considered, coordinated, living answer to what protecting the people you love actually requires, built by you, revisited by you, strong enough to survive the parts of your life you can't yet imagine.

None of this was ever meant to frighten you into action. Fear makes people sign things quickly, and quickly is rarely how good decisions get made. What this book has asked of you, instead, is attention — the same steady attention Josefina brought to her own plan, every few years, for decades. The same attention Maria is teaching her children at that kitchen table right now. Not fear. Stewardship.

You don't need another document tonight. You need to know, clearly, what you actually want. The right document, when you're ready, is simply how that decision gets recorded.

Start there.

Every generation inherits something from the one before it — not just money, not just property, but the quality of the decisions made on its behalf, by people who understood that love, carried far enough forward, becomes responsibility. That's what this book has actually been asking of you. Not to remove yourself from the people you love by planning for a day you won't be there. To stay present in their lives for longer than your own life allows — through a decision, made with care, long before it needed to be made.

Notes and Authorities

The stories in this book are fictional composites. The legal and tax principles they illustrate are not. This section identifies the primary authority behind the material legal, tax, and regulatory propositions in each chapter. It does not cite narrative observations, reflections, or ordinary editorial commentary — only propositions a reader might reasonably rely on. Laws, thresholds, and figures change; each note reflects the law as of this book's publication date and should be reconfirmed before being relied upon.

Chapter 2 — Why a Trust, Not Just a Will

Statutory compensation for the ordinary services of a personal representative and estate attorney is calculated as a percentage of the estate's appraised value under Cal. Prob. Code §§ 10800, 10810. Simplified probate alternatives for smaller estates and a primary residence are addressed at Cal. Prob. Code §§ 13100–13116 (personal property affidavit), § 13200 (real property of small value), and § 13151 (primary residence petition, added by AB 2016, effective April 1, 2025).

Chapter 3 — Who Decides When You Can't

Execution requirements for a valid California power of attorney are set out at Cal. Prob. Code §§ 4121–4122. Automatic revocation of a former spouse's designation as attorney-in-fact upon dissolution or annulment is governed by Cal. Prob. Code § 4154.

Chapter 4 — Your Voice in the Room You're Not In

The default hierarchy of health care decision-makers when no agent has been named is set out at Cal. Prob. Code § 4712. Execution requirements for a valid advance health care directive appear at Cal. Prob. Code §§ 4673–4674. Automatic revocation of a former spouse's designation as health care agent upon dissolution or annulment is governed by Cal. Prob. Code § 4697. Federal privacy protections and the "personal representative" framework are set out at 45 C.F.R. § 164.502(g); see also U.S. Department of Health and Human Services guidance on personal representatives (hhs.gov/hipaa).

Chapter 5 — The Quiet Mistakes

California's rule revoking certain nonprobate transfers to a former spouse, and its express exclusion for life insurance, appears at Cal. Prob. Code § 5040. Employer-sponsored retirement plans subject to joint-and-survivor annuity and spousal-consent requirements are governed by 29 U.S.C. § 1055; the scope of covered plans is defined at § 1055(b). IRAs generally are not subject to that same federal framework. California community property principles affecting marital assets are governed by the Family Code's community property provisions generally.

Chapter 6 — When Family and Money Meet

The 2026 federal annual gift tax exclusion ($19,000 per recipient) and lifetime basic exclusion amount ($15,000,000 per individual) reflect current IRS guidance and are subject to change; Form 709 filing requirements arise under 26 U.S.C. § 6019. Below-market and interest-free loans, including the tax treatment of forgone interest, are governed by 26 U.S.C. § 7872, which applies differently depending on loan type, amount, term, and purpose; a $10,000 de minimis exception applies to certain gift loans but does not apply where a principal purpose is tax avoidance or where proceeds fund income-producing assets.

Chapter 7 — Recognizing the Predators

Financial abuse of an elder or dependent adult, and the civil remedies available, are defined at Cal. Welf. & Inst. Code § 15610.30. Investment professional registration can be verified through FINRA BrokerCheck (brokercheck.finra.org).

Chapter 8 — When Relationships Change

Automatic revocation of specified will provisions benefiting a former spouse is governed by Cal. Prob. Code § 6122. Automatic revocation of certain nonprobate transfers, with express exceptions including life insurance, is governed by Cal. Prob. Code § 5040. Automatic revocation of a former spouse as financial power-of-attorney agent and as health care agent is governed, respectively, by Cal. Prob. Code §§ 4154 and 4697 (see also Chapters 3 and 4). The effect of California's automatic revocation rules on a former spouse's nomination as successor trustee within a standalone revocable trust is not addressed uniformly by these statutes and depends on the specific trust instrument and applicable law; this book does not take a position on that unresolved question, and Chapter 8's narrative is constructed so that its lesson does not depend on one.

Chapter 9 — Lawsuits, Liability, and the Role of Insurance

The California homestead exemption is governed by Cal. Code Civ. Proc. § 704.730, with the protected amount tied to the countywide median sale price for a single-family home in the preceding calendar year, subject to a statutory floor and ceiling. A revocable living trust provides no protection from the settlor's own creditors during the settlor's lifetime, since the settlor retains the power to revoke and reclaim trust assets. Voidable transfers made with actual intent to hinder, delay, or defraud a creditor, or without receiving reasonably equivalent value while insolvent, are governed by California's Uniform Voidable Transactions Act, Cal. Civ. Code § 3439.04, with a good-faith transferee defense at § 3439.08.

Chapter 10 — Working With the Tax Landscape

The federal basic estate and gift tax exclusion for 2026 is $15,000,000 per individual. Portability of a deceased spouse's unused exclusion generally requires a timely federal estate tax return; a simplified method for certain late portability elections, available to estates not otherwise required to file, is provided under IRS Revenue Procedure 2022-32. Step-up in basis for inherited property, including the community property double step-up available to qualifying property under California law, reflects general federal basis-adjustment principles under 26 U.S.C. § 1014. California imposes no separate state estate or inheritance tax and has not since 2005; an estate or trust may nonetheless have its own California fiduciary income tax filing obligation under Form 541 if it meets the Franchise Tax Board's gross or net income thresholds (ftb.ca.gov). Rules governing the timing of required distributions from an inherited retirement account were substantially changed by the SECURE Act and clarified by IRS final regulations issued in 2024 (T.D. 10001); this book deliberately does not state the current mechanics in the body text, as they remain a common source of penalty exposure and are best confirmed directly with a tax professional at the time of inheritance.

Chapter 11 — Blended Families

A stepchild does not automatically inherit from a stepparent under California's intestacy rules based on the relationship alone; California recognizes limited statutory and equitable exceptions, including the statutory adoption doctrine at Cal. Prob. Code § 6454 (relationship beginning during minority, continuing through both lifetimes, and clear and convincing evidence the stepparent would have adopted but for a legal barrier) and the judicial doctrine of equitable adoption preserved at § 6455. See also *Estate of Martino* (2023) 96 Cal.App.5th 596.

Chapter 12 — Planning for the Next Generation

A California parent may nominate a guardian in a will or other signed writing under Cal. Prob. Code § 1500; the court retains the appointment role under Cal. Prob. Code § 1514 and the child-custody standards it incorporates. Whether a trust is counted as an available resource for SSI eligibility, and how trust distributions are treated, is governed by the Social Security Administration's Program Operations Manual System (POMS), principally SI 01120.200 and SI 01120.201. This book addresses third-party special needs trusts funded with a parent's assets; first-party trusts involve different rules and are not covered here.

Chapters 13–15

No material legal propositions in these chapters require citation beyond those already noted in earlier chapters (business succession structures, professional roles, and review practices discussed in Chapters 13 through 15 are presented as practical guidance rather than statutory requirements).

Scan the QR code for more information and working materials

www.protectwhatyouveearned.com

www.ingramcontent.com/pod-product-compliance
Lightning Source LLC
LaVergne TN
LVHW020235210926
848481LV00016B/2331